THEN & NOW

HAVRE DE GRACE

OPPOSITE: This cannon marks the site of the battery on Concord Point. Inscribed on the plaque is: "John O'Neill served the guns single-handed during the British attack upon Havre de Grace on May 3, 1813 until disabled and captured. He was released from the British frigate *Maidstone* through the intercession of his young daughter, Matilda, to whom British Admiral Cockburn presented his gold-mounted snuff box as a token of her heroism." (Courtesy of the Historical Society of Harford County.)

THEN & NOW

HAVRE DE GRACE

Linda Noll

For my husband, Rick, for his encouragement and support during the writing of this book.

ISBN 978-0-7385-9218-3

Library of Congress Control Number: 2011935451

Published by Arcadia Publishing
Charleston, South Carolina

Printed in the United States of America

For all general information, please contact Arcadia Publishing:
Telephone 843-853-2070
Fax 843-853-0044
E-mail sales@arcadiapublishing.com

Visit us on the Internet at www.arcadiapublishing.com

On the Front Cover: The Spencer-Silver Mansion, now a bed-and-breakfast, is located at the corner of Bourbon Street and Union Avenue. John Spencer (at one time, spelled Spenser; however, records do not indicate when the spelling was changed) purchased the property in 1896. However, Spencer's story is rather brief. In 1917, he sold the place at auction to Charles Silver, a canning magnate. Charles Silver cared for the mansion until his death in 1947. Francina (Hopkins) Silver, the widow of Charles, continued to live in the mansion for another 12 years until she sold it to Dr. Edward Simon, a local family physician. Much to her dismay, Simon converted the mansion to apartments and made numerous changes to the interior. Carol Nemeth, the current owner, purchased the property in 1987 and has managed to reconvert and restore some of the interior to its original condition. (Then image courtesy of the Historical Society of Harford County; now image courtesy of the author.)

On the Back Cover: Pictured here is the Susquehanna Hose Company, organized on January 24, 1902, with 33 charter members and incorporated in 1922. Equipped at first with hand-drawn apparatus, the company became motorized between 1910 and 1920. The Burns Carriage Factory fire on September 16, 1902, was the first major alarm for the eight-month-old company. (Courtesy of Susquehanna Museum at the Lock House Archives.)

Contents

Acknowledgments

I would like to thank everyone who has been involved with the writing of this book. I sincerely appreciate all of the interviews, phone calls, emails, and time spent in answering all of my questions and in providing all of the wonderful photographs to make this book possible. Without their assistance, the completion of this book would not have been possible.

Thanks to Richard Sherrill, head of archives of the Historical Society of Harford County, for sharing his unlimited knowledge of Havre de Grace with me; Dottie Meyer, a volunteer at the society, for locating photographs in the society archives; Maryanna Skowronski, the society's administrator, for her support of this project; and Doug Washburn and Walter Holloway for their expertise in scanning vintage photographs for the book. Thanks to Danyelle Dorsey, executive director of the Susquehanna Museum at the Lock House, for providing access to their archives and for scanning vintage photographs for the book.

Thanks to Jim Wollon for meeting with me on several occasions in his charming office on his farm on Craigs Corner Road. Thanks for the use of his photographs for the "Business District in the 1950s" chapter of this book and for providing documentation for those photographs. They were taken over the holiday break (1959–1960) as part of the city planning course that Jim was enrolled in at the University of Virginia. Thanks to Madelyn and Ellsworth Shank for welcoming me into their home with views of the Chesapeake Bay on a blistering afternoon and answering my numerous questions about Havre de Grace while sipping a glass of refreshing iced tea.

Who better to ask when searching for a property in Havre de Grace than the mail carriers? Thanks to Gardner McCullough (and his father, Elwood McCullough, a retiree of the postal system), Sandie Cassady, and Naomi Diggin for their assistance in locating several properties. Thanks to Mary Lambert for telling me about her beautiful home, one of the "sister houses" on Union Avenue, and to John Muldoon of the Vandiver Inn, to Ron Browning of the La Cler D'Or Guesthouse, Carol Nemeth of the Spencer-Silver Mansion, and to Dr. Louis Silverstein for sharing the history of their properties with me. And thanks to Cindy Height of the Art Union, Bob Magee, and Betty Angelucci for their assistance regarding historical properties in Havre de Grace. I appreciate their time.

A special thanks to my family for their understanding and encouragement throughout the writing process, especially when I said, "I have to work on my book! Now! I can't put it off any longer!" And I would then disappear into my office. I extend a special thank you to my editors at Arcadia, Brinkley Taliaferro, Lindsay Carter, and Elizabeth Bray for working with me on this project.

And lastly, thanks to all of those people who had the foresight to take photographs and preserve them for generations to come, whether safeguarding them in your homes or by donating them to the local historical society, and to all of the property owners in the historic city of Havre de Grace who have preserved and restored their structures. It was a pleasure snapping all of the "now" photographs of this beautiful historic city for my book.

INTRODUCTION

The first recorded settlement of the land now known as Havre de Grace was on July 19, 1658, when the Lord Proprietor of Maryland assigned it to Godfrey Harmer, who in turn named it Harmer's Town. On June 30, 1659, the land was reassigned to Thomas Stockett, who then renamed it Stockett's Town. The settlement grew slowly during the next 30 years, and on August 13, 1688, the site was transferred by deed to Jacob Looten. Since this tract of land rests at the head of the Chesapeake Bay where it meets with the Susquehanna River, a ferry for crossing the river became a necessity. In 1695, the first ferry with approved toll rates began operation. Thereafter, the town became known as Susquehanna Lower Ferry. In 1714, the site was sold to John Stokes, who sold lots to individuals. By 1773, the town recorded a population of approximately 200 people.

How did it happen that the name changed from Susquehanna Lower Ferry to Havre de Grace? Some say that the Marquis de La Fayette, a French army officer who played a significant role in the American Revolution, suggested the name. On one of his journeys through Harford County in the late 1700s, he sought overnight lodging at the Rodgers House on his way to Philadelphia. He was very impressed by the beauty of the waterfront settlement and its resemblance to his hometown, Le Havre, France. He is said to have exclaimed, "C'est le Havre" (meaning "ah, the harbor!"), and this expression presumably led to the naming of Havre de Grace. However, some people think that perhaps it was Colonel Rodgers Sr., who served in the militia during the Revolutionary War, who liked the sound of the name and thought it would add distinction to the town.

By 1785, Havre de Grace was incorporated as a town with its own government. In 1789, Havre de Grace was seriously considered for the capital of the United States. However, Havre de Grace lost by one vote. During the 1800s, the town continued to grow. Early industries included oyster and crab harvesting, ice cutting and shipping, and commercial fishing. Also, canning houses were built for packing corn and tomatoes. This led to employment for hundreds of people. Around 1840, improvements in transportation with the Susquehanna and Tidewater Canal and the Philadelphia, Wilmington & Baltimore Railroad led to economic growth for the city. This area also became popular for duck hunting. Hunters stayed at hotels and used local guides for hunting, and soon the art of decoy making came into play. As a result, Havre de Grace prospered, and inns, stores, churches, and schools were built. In 1875, Havre de Grace was incorporated as a city with an elected mayor and a six-member city council that still exists today. During the early part of the 20th century, Havre de Grace prospered as a stop for travelers, including gangsters and gamblers en route to New York City. The racetrack referred to as "the Graw" was in operation from 1912 to 1950. Al Capone was reported to have spent time at the Hotel Chesapeake, now known as Chiapparelli's Restaurant. By the end of the 1950s, the racetrack was removed and rights were sold to Pimlico Race Track in Baltimore.

In telling the history of Havre de Grace, it is important to mention its role in the War of 1812. The British had blockaded the ports of the Chesapeake and Delaware Bays, and several towns along those shores were destroyed, including Havre de Grace. At this time, Havre de Grace had approximately 50 log or frame houses and several inns. Also, there were warehouses and wharves along the waterfront. Around sunrise on the morning of May 3, 1813, about 400 British troops attacked, burned, and pillaged the small town. Within two hours, the town lay in ruins. It is recorded that few structures survived: the Aveihle-Goldsborough House, the exterior walls of St. John's Episcopal Church, and the Elizabeth Rodgers House. The *Weekly Register*, a Baltimore paper, printed, "The ruins of Havre of Grace shall stand as a monument to British cruelty. The villainous deed has aroused the honest indignation of every man." John O'Neill, lighthouse keeper, attempted to defend Havre de Grace by continually firing cannons. However, he was captured and held prisoner aboard a British frigate. His life was spared when daughter Matilda pleaded to British rear admiral Sir George Cockburn for his release, and her request was granted.

According to the 2010 census, the city of Havre de Grace boasts approximately 13,000 residents. At that same time, city tourism records reflect that 220,000 people visited Havre de Grace. Visitors have a variety of bed-and-breakfasts, restaurants, coffee shops, antique stores, boutiques, spas, art galleries, and museums from which to choose. The city's own Tidewater Players present Broadway productions in the old opera house. The headwaters of the bay and outlet of the Susquehanna River also provide recreational activities. Several marinas dot the shoreline for boating and fishing, scenic walking trails meander along the old canal path for avid hikers and birdwatchers, and Tydings Park offers picnicking and festivals throughout the summer. A promenade runs along the shoreline from the Lock House to the yacht basin and offers a commanding view of the convergence of the river and the bay. A paddle steamer, *Lantern Queen*, and an oyster dredging skipjack, *Martha Lewis*, offer leisurely tours on the Chesapeake Bay. The main street organization sponsors First Fridays and a seasonal farmer's market in town. In 1987, the central business district was added to the National Register of Historic Places. The city was recently designated as an Arts and Entertainment District by the State of Maryland. No matter what time of year or what outlet you are looking for, Havre de Grace has something for everyone. C'est le Havre!

CHAPTER 1

City Streets

Ontario Street, looking east towards the city of Havre de Grace, is one way to enter the city. Pulaski Highway (Route 40) intercepts Ontario Street; therefore, one cannot continue into town on this particular street. Travelers need to turn right onto Ohio Street and cross Route 40 to pick up Otsego Street. Traveling west away from the city, the road name changes to Chapel Road. (Courtesy of the Historical Society of Harford County.)

Union Avenue, running north to south, is considered one of the main streets in town. Grassy areas and mature trees obscured the homes that lined both sides of the two-lane street. Union Avenue is now a four-lane thoroughfare, but the stately homes and a few churches still line the street. Several businesses are located at the north end of Union Avenue. The photograph shown on this postcard was taken at the intersection at Congress Avenue looking north. (Courtesy of the Historical Society of Harford County.)

This postcard captures a winter scene of Union Avenue looking south towards Tydings Park from the intersection of Union and Congress Avenues. Havre de Grace United Methodist Church is on the left, and St. John's Episcopal (not shown) is on the right. Notice the illumination light that seems to magically hang in mid-air at the intersection. (Courtesy of the Historical Society of Harford County.)

The photograph for this postcard is of Congress Street looking west towards St. Patrick's Catholic Church, which is located on the corner of Congress and Union Avenues. The row of houses built by the Burns brothers still remains, but the trees obscure the view. The steeple of the church can be seen above the tree line. (Courtesy of the Historical Society of Harford County.)

St. John Street is one of the main streets in the downtown business district. The building on the left was once the home of Havre de Grace Banking and Trust but is now occupied by MacGregor's Restaurant. An awning from the restaurant now stretches over the sidewalk, beckoning patrons into the establishment. On the right is Lyons Pharmacy, established in 1894. (Courtesy of the Historical Society of Harford County.)

Ice gorges in 1904, 1907, and 1910 jammed the Susquehanna River and subsequently flooded the communities along its banks. Since dams were built upriver, there have been no more ice gorges. This is a photograph of Water Street during the 1904 flood. Price's Seafood, established in 1944 and known for its excellent steamed crabs, is farther down on the left. The old warehouse, still partially standing and displaying "Carter's Liver Pills" on the roof, was the location of the Abbott Ice Company. (Courtesy of the Susquehanna Museum of Havre de Grace at the Lock House.)

CHAPTER 2

Historic Houses

This photograph was taken in front of two houses next to the present location of the Methodist Episcopal Church now known as Havre de Grace United Methodist Church on Union Avenue. These houses have been replaced by the "Sister Houses" shown on page 29. Notice the large unicycle and the two gentlemen posing for this photograph, which probably dates to the early part of the 20th century. (Courtesy of Jim Wollon.)

The Aviehle-Goldsborough House, built by Jean Baptiste Aviehle in 1801, is located at 300 North Union Avenue at the corner of Green Street. He purchased the entire block along Union Avenue between Green and Franklin Streets for $400 in 1803. The house exhibits significant French architectural details, including roof and nails. He sold the property to Howes Goldsborough for $1,500 to cover some outstanding debts. The Goldsborough family lived there until 1855. This house is thought to be one of the oldest structures in Havre de Grace and one of few to survive the burning of the city in 1813. It is listed in the National Register of Historic Places. (Courtesy of Jim Wollon.)

The Sappington-Lynn House, at 212 South Union Avenue, was built in 1838 in the Grecian style. It is referred to as one of the "canal houses" because of their origin dating to 1840, when the canal opened. They were constructed of bricks and expensive building materials. The white picket fence is gone. Renovations include three windows at the roofline, shutters that have been removed, and the porch roofline that has been extended. The two lower windows have been replaced with a bay window and two side windows. (Courtesy of the Historical Society of Harford County.)

The Silverstein House, located at 414 Congress Avenue, was owned by Joseph Silverstein. Originally from New York City, Silverstein moved to Havre de Grace in 1937 and opened a clothing store (Joseph's Department Store) in the old Mitchell Motors dealership building at 124 North Washington Street. His son Eli took over the business when his father passed away. The house has remained in the Silverstein family under the ownership of another son, Dr. Louis Silverstein, who runs a family practice in the city. The original cupola was removed in 1940 and an exact replica was installed c. 2003. (Courtesy of the Historical Society of Harford County.)

The A. Lincoln Lyons House is located on the corner of Washington and Commerce Streets near City Park (now known as Tydings Park). It was the home of Dr. Lyons, who opened a pharmacy at 328 St. John Street in 1894. In this postcard, one can see the stone pillars of the entranceway to the park. Trees obscure a major part of the house, and the awnings are no longer there. (Courtesy of the Historical Society of Harford County.)

The Sentman family residence is located at 820 Ontario Street, between Route 40 and Juniata Street. It is believed that the family owned a building supply store in town. The shutters have been removed, the porch has been renovated, and the white picket fence has been replaced with wrought iron. (Courtesy of the Susquehanna Museum of Havre de Grace at the Lock House.)

It is believed that Dr. Richard A. Smith built this house at the corner of Union Avenue and Green Street in 1890. This photograph shows a completed Smith House and one next to it still under construction. Neither house remains today. The property is a vacant lot next to Office Centre. (Courtesy of the Historical Society of Harford County.)

This building once served as a house and store on the southwest corner Adams and Otsego Streets. Once a typical store with a corner entry, this building now consists of several apartments. In the photograph, the unidentified owner and his family stand outside the corner entrance. This entrance and the side porch are no longer there. The sunburst pattern above the top left windows is the only significant architectural feature that still remains. (Courtesy of the Historical Society of Harford County.)

Once the residence and dental office of Dr. Alexander Koser at 114 and 115 St. John Street, these two adjoining structures have undergone significant changes. Today, there is a brick and siding facade with five bays in length, steep pitched roof, and shuttered windows on the second floor. The property today serves as Coakley's Pub & Restaurant, and its current address is 406 St. John Street. (Courtesy of the Historical Society of Harford County.)

Before its demolition, this house was considered the oldest house in Havre de Grace and once stood at the corner of Washington and Bourbon Streets. The Flemish bond brick pattern, belt course at the second floor line, six-panel door, and nine-over-six windows are features indicative of its very early date. The second house to the right could be the newly renovated section of the house shown in the photograph below. (Courtesy of Jim Wollon.)

This frame house with board-and-batten siding on a stone foundation is no longer standing on the corner of Pennington Avenue and Lodge Lane in the business district. There is a white block garage on the property now owned by the Avenue Stained Glass Studio. The Greater Havre de Grace Chamber of Commerce and Havre de Grace Visitor's Center are located across the street. (Courtesy of Jim Wollon.)

The Eldon Leitheiser House no longer remains on Union Avenue next to St. John's Episcopal Church. The house was demolished so that a parish hall and rectory could be built next to the church. Leitheiser attended Havre de Grace High School and the University of Maryland. Later, he served as a director of the First National Bank in Havre de Grace. In the background of the above photograph, one can see St. John's Towers, a retirement facility. (Courtesy of Jim Wollon.)

These homes are referred to as "Sister Houses" and were built in the Queen Anne style of the Victorian period. The owner of the property built these houses as wedding gifts for his children. The one on the left was built in 1893 for his daughter and the house on the right in 1898 for his son. The present owners, members of the Lambert family, restored the houses to their original colors. (Courtesy of Jim Wollon.)

The Gabriel Christie House is no longer standing at Otsego and Ohio Streets. Christie was born in 1756 and served both in the US Congress and in the Maryland Senate. He married Priscilla Hall, daughter of John Hall of Cranberry. In 1783, he petitioned for a charter to build the canal and assisted in the layout and design of the city of Havre de Grace. The house was vacant and in a state of disrepair when this photograph was taken in 1930. Today, a Pizza Hut is located nearby. (Courtesy of Jim Wollon.)

CHAPTER 3

Places of Worship

This granite monument, bearing two quotes from Genesis, marks the location of the first Roman Catholic church in Havre de Grace, which began services in 1844. There are no visible signs of the building, but it is believed to have been a frame structure. This church is believed to have been the predecessor of St. Patrick's Catholic Church. In the adjoining cemeteries, Mount Erin and St. James the Less, many tombstones bear the names of Italian and Irish families who immigrated to Havre de Grace during the mid- to late 1800s. (Courtesy of the Historical Society of Harford County.)

St. Patrick's Catholic Church, at 615 Congress Avenue, is actually the third location for this church. The church initiated services at Mount Erin Cemetery c. 1847 and then moved to a new building on Stokes Streets. The cornerstone for the current building was laid on August 5, 1907, and formally dedicated on July 28, 1908. The church property now includes St. Patrick's Hall, a rental hall with a 350-person capacity suitable for weddings, parties, and more. The church sponsors a Homecoming Program, a free, confidential, and professional assessment and counseling service for returning soldiers and their families. (Courtesy of the Historical Society of Harford County.)

St. Patricks Catholic Church, Havre de Grace, Md.

This is believed to be the first location of the Methodist church in Havre de Grace. The people standing on the front porch are perhaps the minister, his wife, and their children. Most likely, services were held in the home at the time of the church's beginning. Later, the church moved to Union Avenue, then to the corner of Union and Congress Avenues, where it still stands today. (Courtesy of the Susquehanna Museum of Havre de Grace at the Lock House.)

This is the second location of the Methodist Episcopal Church, constructed in 1857 on Union Avenue prior to the structure on the opposite page. This three-story brick building contained a sanctuary on the second floor, and blind round arches may still be seen in the side walls. The building's facade was changed to its present appearance in 1906, when George Borneman purchased the property and converted the space to apartments. (Courtesy of the Historical Society of Harford County.)

The former Methodist Episcopal Church (now known as Havre de Grace United Methodist Church) is located at 101 South Union Avenue. William Plack, a noted architect from Philadelphia, built the church of granite and limestone in 1901–1902. The new building was a gift to the community by canning magnate and banker Stephen J. Seneca, who emigrated from Switzerland. In the postcard, the steeple has not yet been added. The church has two square towers, and the slate roof is trimmed in copper. (Courtesy of the Historical Society of Harford County.)

The congregation of the Presbyterian church arrived in Havre de Grace in 1841, and within two years, it constructed a simple frame building in the Greek Revival style for its worship at 552 Franklin Street. It is the same basic building used today with some extensions and modifications, including a white brick facade. (Courtesy of the Historical Society of Harford County.)

St. John's Episcopal Church, the city's oldest church, is located at the corner of Union and Congress Avenues (114 North Union Avenue). The congregation of this church dates back to 1809. William Stokes donated land for the construction of a church. After a fire in 1832, the church was rebuilt in 1833. The stuccoed panels represent the bottoms of the former second-story windows before the fire. It is one of the city's oldest surviving structures. The rectory in the rear is now St. John's Towers, a retirement facility. (Courtesy of the Historical Society of Harford County.)

Grace Reformed Episcopal Church is an orthodox church in the Anglican tradition. Located at 560 Fountain Street, the church celebrated its 100th anniversary in December 2011. The church supports various missionary programs and participates in Grace Place, a local community organization that benefits the less fortunate. (Courtesy of the Susquehanna Museum of Havre de Grace at the Lock House.)

CHAPTER 4

Hotels, Inns, and Taverns

The Spencer-Silver Mansion, featured on the cover, is now a bed-and-breakfast and is a fine example of high Victoriana. Stained glass, elaborate woodwork, curved glass in the tower, and colored marble and brass decorations around the fireplaces set this house apart from its neighbors. It was built with the latest gas and electric lighting, humidifiers in the gas fireplaces, and Italian marble fixtures. (Courtesy of the Historical Society of Harford County.)

The Harford House was a major hotel during the mid-1890s at the point where St. John Street meets Union Avenue. This hotel was known for its fine kitchen and good accommodations. Attached to the hotel were a dining room, kitchen, and laundry. The laundry faced onto Union Avenue. South of the dining room was a barbershop. This photograph was taken as one looked south from the intersection of St. John Street and Union Avenue. (Courtesy of the Historical Society of Harford County.)

Harford County Land records show that the Havre de Grace Ferry Company purchased this property at Union Avenue and Warren Street from William B. Stokes in 1818. Records indicate that "the brick tavern lately burnt down" stood on the property, most likely damaged when the British attacked Havre de Grace in 1813. The location and unusual size (45 by 50 feet) suggest that this structure was built as a hotel and not as a private dwelling shortly after its purchase in 1818. In 1834, Abraham Jarrett Thomas purchased the property, and in 1856, the Philadelphia, Wilmington & Baltimore Railroad purchased the property and ran it as the Lafayette Hotel until 1922. Several owners continued to operate it as the Lafayette Hotel until 1947, when the property was sold to the Joseph L. Davis Post 47 of the American Legion. (Courtesy of the Historical Society of Harford County.)

The Elizabeth Rodgers House is a Federal-era townhouse and one of the few structures that survived the 1813 burning of Havre de Grace. In 1788, Colonel John Rodgers Sr., who served in the militia during the Revolutionary War, purchased the house and opened a tavern there. His wife, Elizabeth, inherited the property upon his death. Gen. George Washington stayed there on several occasions, as noted in his diary: "crossed the Susquehanna and dined at Havre de Grace at the house of one Rodgers . . . Sept. 20, 1787." (Courtesy of the Historical Society of Harford County.)

The Henry Harrison Hopkins House, located on the corner of Union Avenue and Green Street, was built c. 1868 during the post–Civil War gilded age. The house remained in the Hopkins family (relatives of Johns Hopkins associated with the Johns Hopkins Hospital and University) until Dr. Folweiler, a local eye doctor, took up residence during the 1960s. In 1983, he sold the house to Antonio Barcelone and Eugene Unger, officers of a savings and loan in New Jersey. Unger was charged with embezzlement of $6 million, and subsequently, the house was sold at auction. Ron Browning, current owner, purchased the property at auction and now operates a guesthouse there. (Courtesy of the Historical Society of Harford County.)

The Old Ordinary at Congress Avenue and St. John Street was built in 1814 as an inn offering lodging to weary travelers. It is believed that George Bartol, a town commissioner, ran a tavern here in the early 1800s. The architecture of the building suggests a French Colonial influence with hipped roof and the two-story piazza of this two-and-a-half-story building. Standing on ground level are several African American women, who appear to be more focused on the children than the view of the Susquehanna River afforded by the location. In the 1930s, the building served as a club where African Americans were allowed. (Courtesy of the Historical Society of Harford County.)

Here is another view of the Old Ordinary. Hanging from the corner of the veranda is a National Beer sign. Whether it was serving as a tavern at the time of this photograph (between 1931 and 1940) is not clear. Today, the building is the site of a real estate agency and law offices. The National Beer sign is gone, and the marker reads "the Old Chesapeake Hotel . . . Corporate Offices of A&M Properties and Stark & Keenan Law Offices." (Courtesy of Jim Wollon.)

The Hotel Chesapeake & Restaurant opened here in 1896. During the early 1900s, it was a very popular place to stay when the racetrack known as the "Graw" was one of the most well-known and most frequented tracks in the country. Notables such as Al Capone stayed at the Chesapeake while visiting the Graw. During this time, the first floor was a restaurant and the upper floors served as hotel rooms. Since that time, it has been known as the Crazy Swede, Ken's Steak & Rib House, and is now called Chiapparelli's of Little Italy, owned by Brian Chiapparelli and Ken Beyer. (Courtesy of the Historical Society of Harford County.)

Once the old Colonial Hotel, this building now serves as doctors' offices adjacent to Harford Memorial Hospital at the corner of Union Avenue and Revolution Street. The hotel claimed to be "the largest and best kept hotel in Havre de Grace during the 1940s . . . every room with bath or hot and cold water . . . serves excellent meals . . . very convenient to the Havre de Grace Race Track." (Courtesy of the Susquehanna Museum of Havre de Grace at the Lock House.)

Guests at the Vandiver Inn on Union Avenue still love to sit on the front porch of this 1886 Victorian cottage, which now serves as a bed-and-breakfast. Murray Vandiver's political background included serving in the Maryland House of Delegates, as state treasurer, as appointee to the Bureau of Internal Revenue under Pres. Grover Cleveland, and as mayor of Havre de Grace. (The Vandivers were in President Cleveland's wedding party.) Murray Vandiver built the mansion as a wedding gift to his wife, Annie Clayton Vandiver. Their son Robert lived there until the mid-1960s, when it was converted to apartments. In 1987, local developer A.J. Fair and his wife, Pat, remodeled and reopened the mansion as a bed-and-breakfast. The current owners, John and Susan Muldoon, purchased the inn in 2002. (Courtesy of Historical Society of Harford County.)

CHAPTER 5

Recreation and Entertainment

The grandstand at the Havre de Grace Race Track was located a mile south of the Havre de Grace township. The track was in operation from 1912 to 1950 and was affectionately referred to as "the Graw." It was home of some great horses, such as Man o' War, War Admiral (son of Man o' War), and Citation from Calumet Farm, who won the Triple Crown in 1948. After the racetrack closed, the land was purchased for a state military facility. (Courtesy of the Historical Society of Harford County.)

This park was originally called Bayside Park, but its name was changed in the early 1960s to Tydings Memorial Park to honor the city's famous native son, the Honorable Millard E. Tydings. The entrance, through stone pillars, leads to a war memorial. It was erected in 1919 to commemorate the sacrifices of all the young men of Havre de Grace who fought in the Great War. Other veterans' names were added in 1989. (Courtesy of the Historical Society of Harford County.)

The city park band shell is located in Tydings Park. The park is a very popular spot for festivals and other cultural events throughout the summer season. The Fourth of July carnival and fireworks and other seasonal events draw thousands of visitors. The park includes a picnic area, playground, and pavilion and lies adjacent to the City Yacht Basin and the entrance to the promenade. (Courtesy of the Historical Society of Harford County.)

The City Yacht Basin, also known as Bayside Park and now called Tydings Marina, is perched at the mouth of the Chesapeake Bay. It offers a marina and parking facilities for boaters and park visitors. The Promenade Grill offers sandwiches, ice cream, and beverages for boaters and picnickers. (Courtesy of the Historical Society of Harford County.)

Tennis anyone? The old tennis courts at the Bayou Hotel no longer remain but were well used in the heyday of the hotel, which was built in 1917. The Concord Point Lighthouse is seen in the distance in the middle of the photograph. Off to the left but not shown in the photograph is the Havre de Grace Decoy Museum. (Courtesy of the Historical Society of Harford County.)

Located at the mouth of the Susquehanna River, the Concord Point Lighthouse was built in 1827 by John Donahoo, who was born in Harford County in 1786 and served in the Maryland Militia during the War of 1812. Built of Port Deposit granite, it stands 36 feet tall and has 27 steps to the top. It is the oldest lighthouse in continuous operation in the United States. (Courtesy of the Historical Society of Harford County.)

The first lighthouse keeper was John O'Neill, who served until his death in 1838. At least one member of each generation of the O'Neill family kept the light until the property was sold in 1920. This structure served as the keeper's dwelling during that time. Both lighthouse and keeper's dwelling had fallen into a state of disrepair until the Friends of Concord Point Lighthouse restored the properties. (Courtesy of the Historical Society of Harford County.)

The site of the Susquehanna Museum of Havre de Grace at the Lock House stands at the southern terminus of the Susquehanna and Tidewater Canal. In 1840, Crossett & Spahr, who were working under contract for the canal company, built the house. The lock tender's house served as a toll collection office and as a dwelling for the lock tender and his family. The outlet lock is located in front of the lock house. In the 1980s, the lock was de-silted, remnants of the original gates were removed from the lock, and the lock walls were stabilized. In 1982, the restored house (as a museum) opened its doors to the public. (Courtesy of the Susquehanna Museum of Havre de Grace at the Lock House.)

The original Willou movie theater opened in an old harness shop at 327 St. John Street. In 1908, the New Willou Theatre opened next door in this building at 325 St. John Street. It was renamed the State Theatre during the 1930s. It was opened officially in September 1927 by Durkee Enterprises as a one-screen venue with 573 seats. The movie shown on the marquee, *The Girl from Gay Paree*, was also released in 1927. The Evangelistic Church of Deliverance is now located in this building. (Courtesy of the Historical Society of Harford County.)

Susquehanna Lodge 130 of the AF&AM Masonic Temple is located at 215 North Washington Street. Freemasonry is the oldest fraternal organization in the world, open to all men, with suborganizations open to women and families. The organization is dedicated to promoting improvement in the character of its members and to helping those in need. The coffee shop, Jana's Java, is now located on the bottom level. (Courtesy of the Historical Society of Harford County.)

CHAPTER 6

Business Establishments

This building no longer exists, and the property is owned by Harford Memorial Hospital. Whistle Bottling Company was one of the first bottling companies in Havre in Grace. Notice the old delivery trucks parked by the building and the sign on the side of the building: "Thirsty? Just Whistle." Now Pepsi and Coca-Cola have distribution centers in the town. (Courtesy of the Historical Society of Harford County.)

The Susquehanna Hose Company, now located in five houses, is responsible for the fire protection services for the city. Located at the intersection of Pennington and Union Avenues is House Two, the oldest firehouse in Harford County. In this photograph, the firehouse is decorated in stars and stripes, possibly for the Fourth of July parade in town. (Courtesy of the Susquehanna Museum of Havre de Grace at the Lock House.)

The Burns Carriage Factory once stood in this empty lot at 666 Green Street. The business is credited with building the first US mail wagon. By 1907, the factory was shipping products to every state and some foreign countries. No more carriages were built after 1917. When the business closed, the building was turned into apartments. The building suffered a fatal fire on December 25, 1968. (Courtesy of the Susquehanna Museum of Havre de Grace at the Lock House.)

This is the old railroad station for the first railroad through Perryville and Havre de Grace, called the Philadelphia, Wilmington & Baltimore (PW&B). After the Civil War, the tracks were relocated here from Pennington Avenue and the wooden bridge was built. The bridge is no longer there, but the stone pillars remain. In 1881, the Pennsylvania Railroad took over control of the PW&B. The present (1906) bridge was built adjacent to the PW&B structure. In 1976, ownership passed to Amtrak. This area is now known as David Craig Park in honor of the former city mayor and current county executive for Harford County. (Courtesy of the Historical Society of Harford County.)

The old Baltimore & Ohio (B&O) Railroad station was built in the 1880s at the top of a hill on the right side of Ontario Street above Angel Hill Cemetery. This rival railroad of the PW&B was forced to construct a parallel route between Baltimore and Philadelphia across the Susquehanna River. In 1962, the B&O was purchased by the Chesapeake & Ohio, and it became part of the CSX Corporation in 1980. (Courtesy of the Historical Society of Harford County.)

Two men stand on the porch of the Havre de Grace Gas Company. It is not certain where this building was located, but it was possibly at 237 St. John Street. The gas and electric company had been furnishing most of the utility services in Harford County since the late 1920s, when it took over the Havre de Grace Gas Company. The electric company continued to use this location as a place where customers could make inquiries and requests and transact other business with the company. (Courtesy of the Susquehanna Museum of Havre de Grace at the Lock House.)

When Whistle Bottling Company changed its name to Kelly Beverage Company, the exterior of the building also experienced some changes. The outline of the roof and size of the building remained virtually the same; however, the frame facade was replaced with block and shingle. (Courtesy of the Susquehanna Museum of Havre de Grace at the Lock House.)

Prior to its move to the Union Avenue location (shown on opposite page), the post office was located in the McComas Building on the corner of Franklin Street and Union Avenue. The building now has a ramp to the Franklin Street entrance of the Painted Lady shop. Vancheries and a dry-cleaning business occupy the space facing Union Avenue. (Courtesy of the Historical Society of Harford County.)

A large Victorian house once stood at this location before the WPA built this structure in 1936 to serve as a post office. Serving on the project were architect Louis Simon and engineer Neal Melick. The post office outgrew this facility and moved to a more spacious one on Juniata Street in the 1990s. The building is now the home of the Susquehanna Obstetrics-Gynecology-Nurse Midwifery Center. (Courtesy of the Historical Society of Harford County.)

This building once had a third floor until it was destroyed in a fire in 1921. The offices for city hall were located here until a new structure was built on Pennington Avenue. On the second floor, the City Opera House was showing movies by 1908 and was in full operation by 1917. It continued to show movies until 1929. Rumor has it that Durkee Enterprises (who owned the State Theatre) leased the rival house in order to eliminate the competition. Today, it is home to the productions of the Tidewater Players. (Courtesy of the Historical Society of Harford County.)

The First National Bank was incorporated in 1883 just two doors down from this location at 321 St. John Street. In 1908, noted architect William Plack designed this building, which is an adaptation of an 18th-century English gatehouse. The bank closed its doors in 1958, and this was the site of several retail properties before it was converted to a banquet hall, La Banque de Fleuve, in 2008. (Courtesy of the Historical Society of Harford County.)

Once the M.J. Kelly Clothing Store, this property in the 100 block of North Washington Street is now home to a State Farm Insurance sales office. On the left is the Dutch Boy Paint Center, and to the right, Karen's Natural Market shares the building with the insurance office. (Courtesy of the Susquehanna Museum of Havre de Grace at the Lock House.)

The Joseph Good & Son house and store is located at 500–552 Franklin Street, opposite the Presbyterian church. Built in 1893 and owned and operated by the Good family for several generations, this is a fine example of a storefront house. Havre de Grace had a collection of what was called "storefront houses." These buildings were usually built in residential neighborhoods and served both as homes and workplaces for family businesses. (Courtesy of the Historical Society of Harford County.)

From 1910 to 1944, the Harford Memorial Hospital was located in this lovely 20-room Victorian home at the corner of Union Avenue and Revolution Street. The Victorian home was designed by noted Baltimore architect George A. Frederick, who also designed the city hall in Baltimore City, Maryland. At that time, the population of Harford County was about 29,000, whereas today, it is about 250,000. The brick building here today is a newly renovated facility with 105 beds and offers acute care with a full complement of medical, diagnostic, and emergency care services. (Courtesy of the Historical Society of Harford County.)

The original Havre de Grace High School was built in 1896 at another location. The current school was established in 1955, and the primary structure was built in 1961 at the corner of Juniata Street and Congress Avenue. In 1991, the school was designated a National School of Excellence. The school motto is "Enter to Learn, Leave to Serve." (Courtesy of the Historical Society of Harford County.)

Once the site of the Havre de Grace Race Track, or the "Graw," this 1,000-acre property came under the ownership of State of Maryland in 1951. Today, most of the racetrack is used by the Maryland Army National Guard, and the infield is the venue for community athletic events. Also, Chesapeake Industrial Park is located there and is home to 12 businesses that employ over 1,200 individuals in the local workforce. (Courtesy of the Historical Society of Harford County.)

CHAPTER 7

The Business District in the 1950s

Welcome to Havre de Grace via the old Route 7 cutoff over the railroad bridge. Not too much has changed in this location except that the old steel trusses over the stretch of road that crosses the railroad tracks have disappeared. Continue on this road and the name changes to Revolution Street as it leads into the city. (Courtesy of Jim Wollon.)

Entering Havre de Grace by way of Revolution Street, the old Acme Market is long gone. The business was located on Revolution Street near the intersection at Juniata Street. The Eye Center and other businesses are located there now. (Courtesy of Jim Wollon.)

Another way to enter the business district of the city is to travel on Pennington Avenue. A large three-story house stood at the intersection of Pennington and Union Avenues until it was demolished to make way for the Havre de Grace branch of the Harford County Public Library in 1960. For decades, residents have visited this library, which now boasts over 60,000 volumes of books. (Courtesy of Jim Wollon.)

Continuing east on Pennington across Union Avenue towards the river, Pennington Avenue is a divided highway today; however, this was not the case when the avenue crossed over the railroad tracks. The tracks continued down to the end of Pennington Avenue, where a railroad ferry awaited to offer transportation across the river. The frame structure on the left side of Pennington Avenue has been replaced with a concrete-block garage. (Courtesy of Jim Wollon.)

This is the intersection of Pennington Avenue and St. John Street on the east side of town and the center of the downtown business district. The Robin Hood Café is no longer on the corner. Vincenti Decoys & Collectibles and Amanda's Florist are located on one corner, and the Vineyard Wine Bar is located on the corner across Washington Street. (Courtesy of Jim Wollon.)

Washington Street, looking north from the intersection of Pennington Avenue, is the primary business district of Havre de Grace. A variety of businesses, specialty shops, and restaurants line both sides of the street for an approximately two-block area. The two northern blocks of Washington Street and St. John Street between Warren and Green Streets are considered the commercial district of Havre de Grace. (Courtesy of Jim Wollon.)

In the 100 block of North Washington Street, Tip Top and Bond's Bakeries once delivered bread and cakes to Seibert's Foodland. Washington Street Books and Music now occupies that space. On the corner, Chesapeake Finance offered loans, as the sign on the front of the building indicated: "Cash with speed for every need." After the business closed, the Tattered Barn and Tasteful Touches (gently used furniture) moved in on the bottom level. (Courtesy of Jim Wollon.)

There are two identical brick buildings shown in this photograph. Joseph's Department Store, started by Joseph Silverstein, now occupies the space where Harry Mitchell's automobile showroom once was located. Willie's Barber Shop moved into the old Bucchi Shoe Store space and the Park Plaza Billiards moved in when Siebert's Grocery moved across the street. Java by the Bay, a coffee shop, occupies the bottom level of the building in the center of the photograph. (Courtesy of Jim Wollon.)

At the corner of Pennington Avenue and Washington Street used to be the Chat 'n' Chew, which is now the Vineyard Wine Bar. In this block, stores were located on the bottom level and owners lived above. The Davis Jewelry Store was located on the far right end, Correiri's Fruit Stand was in the middle, and Frank Shoes is now the Advanced Electronics store. (Courtesy of Jim Wollon.)

Greenleaf Supply Company was located on Congress Avenue until it moved to this location on North Washington Street. Still in business today, the store specializes in art supplies, paints, and wallpaper. Bowens & Snyder, Opticians, was located at the south end of the block. During recent years, ice cream and dessert shops such as Sweet William's and the Ritz occupied this space; however, the property is vacant today. (Courtesy of Jim Wollon.)

The old Hecht's Hardware Store stood in this block of Washington Street. Today, Laurrapin Grille occupies that space and the block building next to it. This block building was once a wooden frame structure, as seen next to the Masonic Temple on page 58. The Laurrapin Grille offers a fine array of food and entertainment. Farther down the block to the right is Amanda's Florist. (Courtesy of Jim Wollon.)

An old Read's Store occupied the Rodgers Tavern. This building survived the burning of Havre de Grace in 1813. The Rodgers family had a long history in the town as well as a line of family members who served in the Navy. Commodore John Rodgers served in the War of 1812, his son John served in the Civil War, and great-grandson John served in World War I. The property was purchased by Madelyn and Ellsworth Shank in 1980, and restoration work was done. It still retains the name of the Rodgers House Tavern and offers food, drink, and pool tables for is customers. (Courtesy of Jim Wollon.)

The C.H. Rigler Furniture Store was located in this block of St. John Street until a fire destroyed the building. The space is now an open courtyard for the Rampant Lion Artisan Gallery, featuring works of local artists. To the left is the old First National Bank Building, which is now a banquet hall. (Courtesy of Jim Wollon.)

Once the home of Shafer's Appliances, which sold Zenith and Whirlpool brand appliances as indicated by the sign out front, it is now home to ReMax Elite Realty. McLhinney's News Depot used to be next door to the right. It was the place to catch up on the news around town and only place in town to purchase a copy of the *New York Times*. Blue Earth Leather is now located in that space. (Courtesy of Jim Wollon.)

A parallelogram-shaped building still stands at the south end of St. John Street. An insurance agency was nestled between the August Jewelry Store and the Sears Roebuck & Company on the right. A global fair trade business, Doodads, has replaced the jewelry store, and Sears is long gone. However, Domenick's Barber Shop still remains. (Courtesy of Jim Wollon.)

Located a little north of the Old Ordinary on St. John Street, this building, though in the south end of the business district, actually was once the home of the Gamitora family. The spacious three-story house no longer remains. There is only an empty lot between the Old Ordinary and the house on the far right with the exception of a barbershop. (Courtesy of Jim Wollon.)

Levy's Department Store moved from this location on St. John Street in 1963. Since Lyons Pharmacy owned the building, Dr. A. Lincoln Lyons moved his pharmacy to that space. Established in 1894, Lyons Pharmacy, also known as the Rexall Store, has survived as one of Havre de Grace's oldest businesses. The pharmacy has been a part of the growth and changes in the city, adding a large over-the-counter selection of drug needs, everyday items, gifts, cards, and more. (Courtesy of Jim Wollon.)

At one time, there were two gas stations and two taxi stands at this location at the convergence of St. John Street, Union Avenue, and Warren Street. Montville Taxi, still in operation, was located next to the Amoco, and Coen's Taxi was next to the Gulf station. The buildings are now vacant. The American Legion (once the Lafayette Hotel) is located across the road. (Courtesy of Jim Wollon.)

The old Phillips 66 gas station was located at 911 Pulaski Highway (Route 40). It was open from 7:00 a.m. until 10:00 p.m. daily. No gas is sold here today, but it does offer car repair service. The one-story building has not changed much in appearance; however, the cowboy mascot on the roof has been changed to look more like an auto mechanic and now rests on solid ground. (Courtesy of Jim Wollon.)

This area by the riverfront is now home to the Frank Hutchins Memorial Park and is located at the end of Congress Street on the banks of the Susquehanna River. This two-acre waterfront park offers a fishing pier, benches, and parking. In 1977, Frank Hutchins was mayor of the city, and he accepted the deed transfer of the lighthouse from the United States, conditional upon the city maintaining the light. This park was named in his memory. (Courtesy of Jim Wollon.)

This area once served as the city dump and was located just within city limits off Graceview Drive. At one time, the B&O train bridge was visible, as shown in this photograph, but it is not today. The tree line has obscured what was once a beautiful view of the river and the bridge. This site is now the home of the Havre de Grace Community Center. (Courtesy of Jim Wollon.)

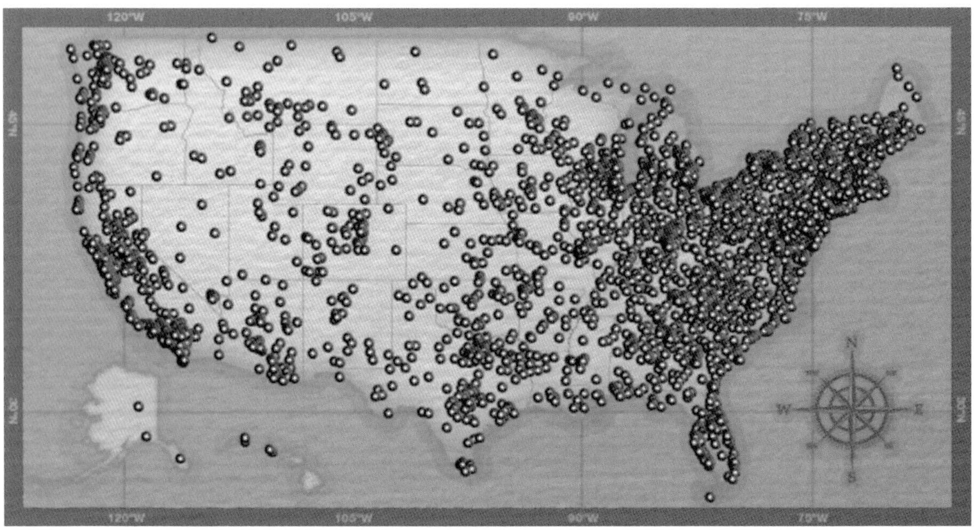